I0478438

Act Next!
5 MORE Action Steps To Take Immediately
To Move Your Business Forward

By Charlene L. Parlett, AAM, CPS

Copyright © 2017
Seamless Properties, LLC

Act Next! 5 More Action Steps To Take Immediately To Move Your
Business Forward

Written By
Charlene L. Parlett

Copyright © 2017 Seamless Properties, LLC

All names, characters, businesses, places, events and incidents are
either the products of the author's imagination or used in an
illustrative manner only.

All rights reserved. No part of this book may be reproduced or
transmitted in any form or by any means, electronic or mechanical,
including photocopy, recording, or any information storage and
retrieval system, without permission in writing from the author.

Library of Congress Cataloging-in-Publication Data
Parlett, Charlene L.1969 –
Act Now! 5 Action Steps To Take Immediately To
Move Your Business Forward/non-fiction/by Charlene L. Parlett
ISBN-13: 978-1546511557
ISBN-10: 1546511555
BUS060000 BUSINESS & ECONOMICS / Small Business
1. Non-Fiction, American I. Title.

Cover Illustration Copyright © 2017 by Seamless Properties, LLC
Book Design and Production by Createspace

Formatted and/or Printed in the United States of America

TABLE OF CONTENTS

ACKNOWLEDGEMENTS

Your beginnings will seem humble,
so prosperous will your future be.
The Bible: Job 8:7 NIV

I am truly humbled and grateful for everyone who has been a part of the writing of this second book in the Act Now! Series. So many people have been a part of this process by sharing their own stories of business ownership – often success and failure – and then rising out of the rubble to succeed again.

To my clients - thank you for partnering with me. I learn as much from you as I hope you learn from me each day. Each one of you is woven into my writings and part of what I bring to the next seminar, workshop and client.

To my friends and family – you are the support that keeps me moving forward when I start despising my small beginnings. You are also the ones that "keep it real" for me.

To my mentors and coaches – These books come from the abundance you have poured into me. Thank you isn't enough. Your input, advice, knowledge, wisdom and encouragement are why I get to do what I love every day.

Coming January 2018:
Act Again!
Next-Level Action Steps To
Catapult Your Business
The Third Book in the Act Now! Success Series

INTRODUCTION
Why Act Next?

I am a firm believer that people who chose to aim for their future while focusing on their now always come out on top.

But life happens. Often in ways you can't predict and maybe don't want it to. Within a few short years I experienced extensive transitions in my personal, professional and family life simultaneously. I got divorced after 23 years of marriage. I was forced to sell my share of a prosperous business below value and change careers as a result. I started a new business. I lived alone for the first time in 25 years, which led to empty nest syndrome (yes, it's real). And to top it all off I had a health issue that required surgery.

I fell into a severe depression from the stress. There were days when the only reason I got out of bed was to meet with a client or go to a business meeting – or prepare for a visit from one of my adult children.

I don't remember exactly what occurred – perhaps I was listening to a podcast or a mentor on the phone – but something pierced through the thick cloud of deep blue funk.

Get up.

I knew it didn't mean just get out of bed. It meant fight. Get focused again. Get moving again.

Get up.

Every day business owners deal with stress issues the rest of the world knows nothing about. We don't just worry about putting food on OUR table; we worry about making sure everyone who works for us can as well. We deal with the challenges of balancing our business checkbooks and our personal checkbooks. We face the constant struggle of how to keep our business and family lives separate – or not. We are constantly asked for financial help from friends, neighbors, family members and the community, because the world thinks if you own a business you must have plenty of excess cash available. And while I want business owners to *have* plenty of excess cash available, I know most of us simply don't.

Get up.

You didn't go into business just to get by or barely pay your bills. You started your business because you saw it as the path to personal and financial freedom.

Get up.

In **Act Now!** we discussed the first 5 areas that I see as common weak spots for small business owners. Those included:

- **Strategic Planning**

- **Social Media/Internet Presence**

- **Business Contracts**

- **Setting Priorities**

- **Time Management**

With **Act Next!** we will discuss the next 5 areas most small business owners are struggling with.

My goal was to provide you with both practical real-life examples of why these areas are so important, as well as step by step guidance on how to get moving forward.

I want you to thrive and not just survive. Let's get started...

STEP 6
LEADERSHIP

"The challenge of leadership is to be strong, but not rude; be kind, but not weak; be bold, but not bully; be thoughtful, but not lazy; be humble, but not timid; be proud, but not arrogant; have humor, but without folly."
Jim Rohn

There are hundreds of amazing books out there on leadership and you should be reading at least 2 books a year specifically on leadership. As a business owner, YOU ARE A LEADER whether you want the title or not. Your employees and customers look to you for vision, strategy, preparation, education, motivation, growth, value... if you don't bring it at a higher level than the guy who owns your competition you will find yourself losing great people. Take a look at the multiple surveys and tons of statistical data available on workplace satisfaction; "working for a great leader" is always in the top 10. Working for a great leader also translates into "working for a great company" and "having work that is significant/has meaning" because a true visionary leader creates those things as part of the vision.

So here is what I consider **the Top 7 Leadership Traits of a Great Business Leader**. This is NOT a complete list by any means, but it is a starting point for you to evaluate yourself:

1. **Self-Control.** Do you scream, yell, cuss and/or throw stuff around when things go wrong? Do you over-indulge in food, alcohol, cigarettes, excessive sleep, etc. to manage stressful situations? Are your employees or family AFRAID of what you might do when you are angry or stressed? Self-control means that before you worry about having control of your work environment, you learn to control your INTERNAL environment. Being able to address daily challenges in the business realm depends on your ability to control your emotional and physical responses. Being mindful of how your outward reactions affect those around you may be enough to guide you to better responses. For many, working with a professional therapist or counselor for a season can help you develop better habits for managing stress. I personally work with a wonderful therapist on and off to learn how to communicate better and release unnecessary and unhealthy burdens.

2. **Vision for the Future.** Do you have a clear picture of what you want your business to look like, sound like and feel like 20 years from now? What are the big goals you want to achieve? Have you communicated this vision to your employees and customers? As

I said before, people want to be part of something bigger than a paycheck. They want to know their lives have purpose. A vision that communicates more than long term profitability says you truly care about your future, your team and your customers.

3. **Optimism.** If you have self-control and a vision of the future that is worth striving for, you should feel optimistic about what life holds. Great leaders are not delusional; they know the real challenges they will need to face in order to achieve their goals. But they have a plan that gives them certainty of success long-term; even when communicating the challenges it is always with a positive attitude toward it.

4. **Confidence**. I didn't understand how vitally important confidence is for a leader until I started working with Dr. Keith Johnson (America's #1 Confidence Coach, Best Selling Author and Conference Speaker). Dr. Johnson has devoted much of his life to study, apply and teach confidence to leaders world-wide. As he describes it, "Confidence is the fuel that empowers you to maximize your performance, potential and profits. Most people's internal engines are totally shut down. Just like a race car, the only way to

achieve the engine's extraordinary performance is to begin by starting the engine." Developing confidence takes practice. It's normal to feel more confident in certain situations than others. As a leader, confidence needs to be your norm.

5. **Humility**. If your first response was to think that humility and confidence are opposites, I will have to strongly disagree with you on that. One of my mentors and teachers is Dr. John Kelly. Dr. Kelly can best be described as a man with a gigantic presence! Not only is he physically intimidating (he was a professional football player in his youth), but he carries an atmosphere of authority and influence when he enters a room. He is also one of the most humble men I know. In my journal from January 2010 (you don't keep a journal? Get one today and start), I have a note from an event I attended where he defined meekness as "passion under control." This changed my perspective on what it meant to be humble; I began to see that humility was not a position of weakness but of strength. A humble leader recognizes who they truly are, where their strengths lie, and the areas in their life that they need to work on.

6. **Strategy.** If you have a great vision but no plan for how to achieve it, that vision is simply a dream. Imagine being the captain of a large ship trying to cross the Atlantic. You rely on your navigational equipment to keep you steering in the right direction. It also helps you make course corrections and change course in order to avoid a dangerous storm – your navigational equipment, weather monitors, and keen understanding of the ocean are all part of your strategic planning process for getting to your final destination. Without them, a mere 1-3 degrees error will result in you being thousands of miles off course, behind schedule and possibly in danger. As a leader, you need to have a strategic plan in place for your business. How are you going to measure progress? What are the steps you are going to take to get to your next short-term goals? And how do those goals feed the long-term vision? Too many business owners get tossed to and fro by the winds of the day (the news, the latest sales pitch, today's employee drama) and wonder why a year later they are so far off course from where they wanted to be. As the owner, you are the leader, the captain of this ship. You've got to put in place the strategy for success.

7. **Lifelong Learning.** If you want to be a truly extraordinary leader, you have to embrace ongoing education. In the past 100 years, our understand of leading others and managing teams successfully has been transformed by individuals who made the decision to continue to learn, observe, and extrapolate the lessons around them about human psychology and culture into useable information that changed the face of business. Most of my clients get at least 1 book assigned to them during our coaching contract based on their areas of educational need. The skills and knowledge you need to be a business owner are not the same as the ones you need to be a great technician, insurance representative, doctor, lawyer, web designer, etc. Within your technical profession you probably have either required Continuing Education Units or are constantly learning new things in order to stay up to date with the latest and greatest products and services in your industry. The same goes for being an business leader – constantly be earning CEUs that make you a better owner, team manager and leader for the people around you.

ACTION PLAN:

What 3 steps are you going to take within the next 30 days to implement what you learned in this chapter?

1._____

2._____

3._____

STEP 7
COMMUNICATION

"To effectively communicate, we must realize that we are all different in the way we perceive the world and use this understanding as a guide to our communication with others."
Tony Robbins

If you've ever stumbled over your words during a presentation; if you've ever avoided a conversation because it was going to be difficult or awkward; if you've ever had to have "the talk" with one of your children – you understand why great communication skills are so vital!

Talking is not the same as communicating. Have you ever been talking to someone and knew they weren't listening to a word you said? Have you ever zoned out during a conversation?

For true communication to occur, there must be present:

> **Attentiveness.** Active listening is a skill you must develop if you want to be a great communicator. Each person needs to be focused on the topic at hand. That's easy when you are interested in the topic, but it requires conscious effort if you aren't. And let's face it, a lot of necessary communication isn't always

that exciting. But an active listener can actually shift the atmosphere of a conversation. When people see you are truly hearing their heart through their words, they are more likely to open up and hear what you have to say as well.

Engagement. Participate in the communication process. As the listener, this may mean forcing yourself to hear what is being said WITHOUT preparing what you are going to say at the same time. It may mean shifting your body posture to fully focus your attention on who is speaking. It may mean giving verbal cues to indicate you are following along with what is being said. As the speaker, looking for physical cues like eye contact, distraction will help you pull your audience back into the moment. Allow those you are speaking with to share their insights, or grumblings, knowing their input could be valuable to your future success.

Love. Both the speaker and the listener must strive to put the needs of the other above themselves. What you have to say is not nearly as important as the intent behind it. Are you more concerned with making your point or inflating your ego than the well-being of your listener?

NOTE: Be Aware of Critical Conversations. Have you ever started off chatting about something that was pretty low-keyed only to end up in a shouting match and wondering how that happened? In the book <u>Crucial Conversations</u> (which I highly recommend) you learn valuable skills on how to identify when a "crucial" conversation is about to start and the best way to handle them with grace and tact so that true communication and resolution can occur.

If you don't think of yourself as a good communicator, the good news is that there are plenty of resources to learn better communication skills. One of the best options out there is <u>Toastmasters International</u>. Toastmasters International is a club specifically designed to help you develop better public speaking skills. Before you run for the hills screaming because I said, "public speaking," you probably do a lot more public speaking already than you think. Leading a team meeting in your office, presenting an award to an employee, giving a eulogy or a toast are all common public speaking events.

I have been a member of Toastmasters International for several years now. When I started, I didn't have a fear of public speaking, (years as a youth leader and singer took care of that) but I knew I had some bad verbal habits. I said "uh" and "um" too often. I used slang inappropriately. I wanted to be confident speaking in large business seminars and know my skills were polished and engaging. In Toastmasters I found an encouraging, motivating environment of like-minded professionals.

If you want to accelerate your learning and are willing to make the financial investment, another great option is Dale Carnegie courses. Dale Carnegie wrote the famous best seller <u>How To Win Friends And Influence People</u>. Dale Carnegie Training offers a wide variety of specific communication courses and in-depth, immersion courses based on your interests. For more information on these courses, visit <u>www.seamlesscoach.com</u> and download the Act Next! Resources list.

Communication also includes written form. In the first book in this series, **Act Now!**, I discuss several different written communications that are vitally important in a business, including operating agreements, employee contracts and handbooks, and policies and procedures.

ACTION PLAN:

What 3 steps are you going to take within the next 30 days to implement what you learned in this chapter?

1._____

2._____

3._____

STEP 8
PERSONAL HEALTH

*"The foundation of success in life is good health:
that is the substratum fortune; it is also the basis of
happiness. A person cannot accumulate a fortune
very well when he is sick."*
P.T. Barnum

In the blink of an eye a thriving, prosperous business can go bankrupt – and it didn't have to happen.

This trickles down to families losing their primary source of income, vendors having to go to court to get paid a fraction of what they are owed and customers with half-done work struggling to find someone who is willing to complete the job that another service provider started.

It's preventable, or at the very least mitigable. It requires YOU taking care of yourself.

One of the top 5 reasons businesses close their doors after being successful is poor health of one of the owners. If the owner is also one of the primary technical producers, the impact of a health scare is multiplied exponentially.

Most small business owners have several bad habits that put their physical health at risk, including:

- Eating highly processed foods/fast foods several times a week.
- Eating out several times a week.
- Insufficient sleep.
- Failing to make time for annual health exams.
- Ignoring warning signs of health concerns.
- Not taking vacation days.
- Not working out regularly

Sound familiar? I have clients who want to justify their physically demanding work as exercise and on occasion I can agree. If you are hauling 50 lb. bags across a parking lot I can see how that is strength training. But being on your feet all day does not have the impact that focused aerobic and cardio exercise does.

Taking care of your physical health is the #1 priority you must set if you want to be successful long-term.

A healthy body manages stress better. It provides clearer thinking for more effective decision making. It allows you to accomplish more in a day than most people. But it demands TIME. And that is the most frequent excuse I hear.

> *I don't have time to exercise 3 days a week…*
>
> *I don't have time to make my lunch…*
>
> *I don't have time (or energy) to make dinner…*
>
> *I can't get to bed at a decent hour…*
>
> *I can't take time off to go to the doctor…*
>
> *I can't leave on a vacation, the whole business will come to a screeching halt if I do…*

About 5 years into the business, my father went in for a physical; during a stress test the doctors found a serious heart issue that resulted in open heart surgery *a week later*. The doctor told him that he was the perfect example of someone who drops dead one day and nobody knows why – because on the outside he appeared healthy. Since heart disease can be hereditary and my mother died when I was 14 of a heart related issue, this scared the hell out of me. I knew if I didn't want to follow my dad into the operating room a few years down the road I needed to make changes immediately.

During the early years of starting my first business I used every one of the excuses I listed. I was overweight and tired all the time. I ate out for lunch almost every day. I rarely cooked dinner because I was exhausted at the end of a 10-hour day. I was on my feet a lot at work. I didn't want to hear anything negative from the doctor. And I was the Most Valuable Player in the office so my absence left a tremendous hole to fill – a hole I created and failed to train anyone else to handle. I went to bed late after taking care of kids and a home that I felt like I was neglecting while I built the business. And the stress of the business resulted in poor quality sleep.

I didn't want my kids to go through what I went through losing a parent at an early age. And I didn't want to see my business crash because I was in the hospital, unable to work. I had to change.

Here are the steps I took over 24 months (I got one habit in place before starting the next):

- I scheduled my annual health exam and was faithful to go every year.
- I joined a menu planning service and used it to streamline my grocery shopping and meal planning. *This saved me hours, money and stress. For more information on the meal planning service I use, download the Act Next! Resources list at* www.seamlesscoach.com
- I committed to cooking dinner 5 nights a week. *This meant I had to leave the office on time.*

- I packed my lunch at least twice a week – usually leftovers I packed as I cleaned up dinner.
- I bought and read several healthy cookbooks (NOT diet books).
- I hired a trainer that came to my house. *You can't avoid working out when they're knocking on your door.*
- I went to bed on time, every night. *I learned how wonderful melatonin is to help get a good night's sleep.*
- I hired a part-time assistant. *Best decision ever…*
- I started taking 3-day and 4-day "weekend" mini-vacations. *This forced me to prepare my staff to handle things in my absence.*

This is NOT easy and I am not implying that it will be for you. But it is absolutely necessary.

It took me a few years to faithfully put all these habits in place. And over the past 5 years I have experienced the best health in my life. I get up at 5 am most weekdays so that I have time for my morning routine and to work out before starting my day. I eat healthy most of the time – I still splurge on a great cheeseburger occasionally and hot french fries are one of my favorite treats. I go to bed at a decent hour so that I get a full night's sleep. I take 3-

day vacations as often as possible and pre-plan a 7-10 day cruise each year with my family that we look forward to it the whole year. I lost 50 lbs and have energy I never expected. I'm healthier today than in my 20s and 30s.

My business thrived as I took control of my personal health and well-being. My staff appreciated the positive attitude I came to work with. I now hire based on what the business needs to manage workloads and reduce stress across the entire company.

IF I had a severe health concern that required my absence from the business, it would still thrive under the leadership of the people I put in place. Knowing I have done everything I can to make sure my people are secure in their jobs gives me great satisfaction.

Please take your health seriously. Stop making excuses and start making changes.

ACTION PLAN:

What 3 steps are you going to take within the next 30 days to implement what you learned in this chapter

1._____

2._____

3._____

STEP 9
NETWORKING EFFECTIVELY

"First, you have to be visible in the community. You have to get out there and connect with people. It's not called net-sitting or net-eating. It's called networking. You have to work at it."
Ivan Misner, Founder –
Business Network International

Contrary to what some of my business associates would say, I am an introvert. For years I avoided networking as much as possible. Doing a great job and having a great online and word of mouth reputation were enough, right?

Wrong....

My perspective on what networking is and is not were askew. I had two wrong assumptions about networking:

> It's all about the sales pitch; it's about trying to sell the other person...

> Nobody really likes to do it, we just have to...

Effective networking is about building relationships with people. People like to do business with people they like and trust. And by building relationships with others you find opportunities to bring value to others.

Networking is vitally important to your business. Having a great online reputation still can't replace meeting people face to face and giving them the opportunity to see you, not just your logo. I've had people who have never used my services recommend me to others based solely on the fact that they knew me personally, liked me, and trusted me enough to attach their name to mine.

The most successful professional networking organization in the world is Business Network International®(BNI®). The primary core value of the organization is "Givers Gain®." When I became a member and realized networking wasn't about making a sales pitch five minutes after meeting someone but instead about building rapport, relationship, and finding out how I can help them grow their business as well as my own, I became a fan of networking. I could get behind that concept!

That doesn't mean I always love networking events. Walking into a room full of strangers is difficult for me. I set specific goals for who I want to introduce myself to, knowing the most important part is following up after the event.

1. **Join a networking group or public speaking group**. This gives you the opportunity to practice getting comfortable meeting people and sharing what you do on a consistent basis with like-minded individuals.

2. **Attend at least 1 networking event per month**. A good source of events is your local Chamber of Commerce or professional organizations.

3. **Plan ahead**. How many people are you going to meet? What are you going to say? What questions are you going to ask?

4. **Get a professional name tag made**. It should clearly identify your business and name in easy-to-read lettering. Wear it on the right lapel. Why? Because as you shake hands, people naturally follow the line of sight up your arm to that area and can't help reading it.

5. **Arrive early**. Arriving early means I don't have to walk in on a huge group of strangers; I can greet people one at a time at the door. I can scope out the room. This helps introverts like me feel more confident.

6. **Ask if you can help.** As someone who has organized these types of events for years, I can tell you that help is always appreciated. Even if they have everything under control, you'll be remembered for offering.

7. **Ask for an introduction**. If you arrive early and know ahead of time who you want to meet, ask one of the organizers if they can introduce you. If you aren't sure who is in attendance, tell the host what you do and ask if they could recommend someone you should meet. Most of the time they will gladly make the introduction for you.

8. **FOLLOW UP**. This is the most important step. Make sure you get a business card from everyone you meet for the first time. Make notes on it that will help you remember them. Then always follow up with a hand-written note referencing meeting them at the event. Follow up a week later via email or phone call asking to meet for coffee to learn more about what they do. The goal is to build professional relationships. They may or may not be your ideal client, but you might know the perfect client for them, and vice versa. Since so few people follow up, just taking this extra step will make you memorable.

If you take these steps to heart and look at networking with a fresh perspective, you'll come to realize what I have - that often the most productive part of the day is that hour sitting across from someone over a cup of coffee.

ACTION PLAN:

What 3 steps are you going to take within the next 30 days to implement what you learned in this chapter?

1._____

2._____

3._____

STEP 10
ACCOUNTABILITY

"Accountability separates the wishers in life from the action-takers that care enough about their future to account for their daily actions."
John Di Lemme

"You steadily grow into becoming your best as you choose to be accountable and accept responsibility for improvement."
Steve Shallenberger

For most people it's very difficult to stay motivated and on track, even for goals you truly want to achieve. This is particularly true if we are trying to develop a new skill or habit, learn something we haven't learned before, or do something we know we need to do but don't really enjoy doing.

I hate exercising. I know people who LOVE their gym time and can't wait to get there and spend 2 hours grinding away at it. I am not one of those people. I know WHAT to do. I know how IMPORTANT it is that I do it. But until I hired a physical trainer to hold me accountable to my commitment to exercise on a regular and consistent basis, I could not develop the *habit* of exercising.

Most of my clients will tell you that one of the most important aspects they get from the coach-client partnership is the accountability. Some of the changes they need to make in their businesses are HARD. Often those important changes require them to learn something they haven't learned before and feel uncomfortable doing as a result. Knowing their coach is going to call in a week and ask them specifically about their sales for the week, their marketing, what they've done to improve and get momentum, etc. are often the only reason they get them done. And that is OK. Because just like me and exercising, once they are in the habit of doing these things consistently and see the value of it and are able to justify it for themselves, accountability to a third party is a great support mechanism.

If you are not allowing yourself to be accountable to another person for your business to thrive, your chances of success are slim. The most successful business owners have people around them that encourage, motivate, and hold them to what they say they want to achieve. It may be a business coach. It may be a peer advisory group. It may be a mastermind group of fellow business owners. It could be a mentor or close friend with a track record of their own success. All of these are good options – as long as the individual or individuals in a group challenge you to strive for your highest business potential. *If you don't feel a twinge of conviction when you've come up short, or excitement looking forward to telling them about your latest big win, there's no real accountability there.*

Side Note: My opinion is that a couple who own the business together should both attend such a group or be coached together. If only one of you is embracing the accountability element, it doesn't work and can result in conflict between you. I also feel you should have someone other than one another in this role. You are already accountable to your spouse to a great extent – an outside viewpoint can help you work through the next steps for the business without the intimate and emotional ties which may impact the decision-making process.

ACTION PLAN:

What 3 steps are you going to take within the next 30 days to implement what you learned in this chapter?

1._____

2._____

3._____

Moving Forward
Getting Momentum

As a small business owner, you have continuing challenges in front of you on a daily basis. And I want to help. Visit www.seamlesscoach.com today to sign up for my FREE small business tips enewsletter. You can also learn about seminars and webinars we have scheduled to help small business owners increase their cash flow, grow their business, and stay happy doing it!

If you think that working one-on-one with a business coach is the right decision for you, I want to offer you a FREE ONE-HOUR Consultation with a Seamless Coaching Service Coach. Simply fill out the contact form at www.seamlesscoach.com or email info@seamlesscoach.com. Be sure to include your name, business name, phone number and email address to contact you.

Very few people have what it takes to be a successful business owner. It takes more than drive, a strong work ethic, financial stability and a great idea. It takes educating yourself on what works CONSISTENTLY – the principles that have been proven over and over again. My goal is to partner with you to help you learn what you need to know to be successful for decades to come, whether you decide to run the business yourself, pass it down to your kids, or sell it and move on to bigger and better things. *I want to help you thrive, not just survive!*

To Your Success,

Charlene Parlett

Master Certified Business Coach

Helping Exceptional Professionals Become Extraordinary Business Leaders

About Seamless Coaching

Seamless Coaching Service was established in 2006 to provide service based business owners and organizations with education and knowledge necessary for continuing professional success. Seamless Coaching Service is the premier coaching and consulting firm for individual career planning and service-based businesses, serving thousands through coaching, training, seminars, workshops and speaking engagements. Our company, staff and clients strive to live lives of abundance – financially, personally and professionally.

About Charlene Parlett

As an executive coach, published author and certified trainer, our founder and CEO Charlene Parlett is an expert at guiding business owners, corporate executives and managers to become successful leaders. She helps driven people achieve balance in their lives and floundering people find their drive. She has a gift for breaking down the walls between knowledge and action and puts people on the path to success. An expert in conflict resolution and business practices and processes, Charlene is a powerful and professional coach. Her specialties include leadership/soft skills, confidence building, marketing, strategic planning and assisting organizations in developing and implementing best practices. She has worked with coaching organizations to help them develop their own business coaching certification courses. With the publication of her two how-to success books *Act Now!* and *Act Next!* Charlene hopes to help even more business and non-profit leaders achieve their highest potential.

As marketing director of a multimillion dollar independent office supply and furniture company, she played a major role in doubling the company's gross sales by being one of the primary writers on their successful bid for both a state-wide and a federal world-wide government contracts. In 2005, she and her business partner built their service business from dream to delivery, so she understands the challenges businesses faced in real terms. Charlene is passionate about constantly improving on what is great to make it even better and instills that passion in others.

Coming January 2018:
Act Again!
Next-Level Action Steps To
Catapult Your Business
The Third Book in the Act Now! Success Series

Connect With Us Through Social Media

Google
https://plus.google.com/+SeamlessCoachingService
Hinesville

Facebook
https://www.facebook.com/SeamlessCoaching

LinkedIn
http://www.linkedin.com/pub/charlene-parlett-aam/1b/517/322/

Twitter
https://twitter.com/seamlesscoach

For more information on Seamless Coaching Service programs or to book Charlene to speak at your event, visit www.seamlesscoach.com.

Copyright and Trademark Information

This book is protected by U.S. and International copyright laws. The reproduction, modification, distribution, transmission, republication, or display of the content in this book is strictly prohibited without prior written permission from Seamless Properties, LLC. This book is for your use only. You may not give this book away or share it with others. Any trademarked names mentioned in this book are the sole property of their respective companies. None of these companies are affiliated with Seamless Properties, LLC in any way.

Earnings Disclaimer

The information you'll find in this book is to educate you. We make no promise or guarantee of income or earnings. You have to do the work, use your best judgment, and perform due diligence before using the information in this book. Your success is still up to you. Nothing in this book is intended to be professional, legal, financial and/or accounting advice. Always seek competent advice from professionals in these matters. We also recommend that you check all local, state, and federal laws to make sure you are in compliance when using this information. If you break federal, state, city, or other local laws, we will not be held liable for any damages you   incur.

www.ingramcontent.com/pod-product-compliance
Lightning Source LLC
Chambersburg PA
CBHW061229180526
45170CB00003B/1215